The Online Entrepreneur:

Your Comprehensive Guide to Building a Successful Business Online

Walt Smith

CONTENTS

1   The Online Business Landscape   3

2   Identifying Your Niche and Target Market   8

3   Building Your Online Presence   13

4   Developing A Winning Business Strategy   19

5   Driving Online Sales   27

6   Delivering Exceptional Customer Experiences   33

7   Optimizing Operations and Efficiency   40

8   Scaling Your Business   46

9   Innovation and Adaption   53

10 Overcoming Challenges and Embracing Success   60

11 Embracing the Online Business Journey   64

The Online Entrepreneur:
Your Comprehensive Guide to Building a Successful Business Online

INTRODUCTION

Welcome to the transformative world of online entrepreneurship, where the digital landscape offers endless opportunities for building and growing successful businesses. In this book, we present an immersive guide that will equip you with the essential knowledge and strategies needed to navigate the online business realm with confidence and creativity.

The rise of the internet has revolutionized the way we conduct business, opening doors to a global market and enabling entrepreneurs to reach customers far beyond their geographical boundaries. With its low barriers to entry, the online business landscape provides a level playing field for aspiring entrepreneurs to bring their ideas to life and compete with established players in the industry.

In this book, we aim to demystify the intricacies of online entrepreneurship, empowering you to harness the power of the digital world to build a successful business. From the initial stages of identifying your niche and target market to the intricacies of crafting a compelling online presence, we provide practical advice and actionable insights that will help you set a solid foundation for your online venture.

While each online business journey is unique, there are common threads that run through the stories of successful online entrepreneurs. Throughout this book, we will share real-life case studies and success stories, providing you with inspiration and valuable lessons from those who have blazed the trail before you. By understanding their experiences and applying the principles they have discovered, you can avoid common pitfalls and make informed decisions on your path to success. Moreover, we recognize that the digital landscape is ever-evolving, requiring constant adaptation and innovation. We encourage you to embrace a growth mindset, remain agile in your strategies, and stay up-to-date with the latest trends and technologies. By doing so, you will position yourself at the forefront of your industry, always ready to seize new opportunities and navigate the challenges that arise along the way.

As we embark on this journey together, remember that success in the online business realm is not solely determined by profits or recognition. It is also about creating meaningful connections, making a positive impact, and fostering sustainable growth. Throughout this book, we will emphasize the importance of building strong customer relationships, providing exceptional value, and aligning your business goals with your values.

Are you ready to unleash your entrepreneurial spirit and embark on a digital adventure? Join us as we delve into the depths of online entrepreneurship, equipping you with the knowledge, insights, and strategies you need to thrive in the ever-expanding digital marketplace. Get ready to transform your passion into a profitable online business that makes a difference.

At the end of every chapter there will be a note page in case you need to take notes

CHAPTER 1:

THE ONLINE BUSINESS LANDSCAPE

In this compelling chapter, we dive deep into the transformative world of online business, unveiling its immense potential and outlining the key factors that make it an unparalleled platform for entrepreneurial success. The internet has revolutionized the way we conduct commerce, creating a vast and interconnected global marketplace that offers unparalleled opportunities for growth and innovation.

One of the most significant advantages of online business is its ability to level the playing field. Gone are the days when only well-established corporations could dominate the market. Today, even the smallest of enterprises can carve out a niche and compete on a global scale. The internet has shattered barriers to entry, enabling aspiring entrepreneurs to turn their ideas into thriving online ventures.

The reach and accessibility provided by the internet are unparalleled. With just a few clicks, businesses can connect with customers from every corner of the globe, breaking free from the constraints of physical location. This opens up endless possibilities for expansion and growth, transcending traditional boundaries and unlocking a world of untapped potential.

The online business landscape thrives on agility and scalability. Traditional brick-and-mortar establishments often face limitations when it comes to growth, as expanding physical operations can be costly and time-consuming. In contrast, online businesses have the flexibility to adapt and scale rapidly, seizing new opportunities and quickly responding to changing market dynamics. This dynamic nature allows entrepreneurs to capture emerging trends and capitalize on them before traditional businesses can even react.

Moreover, the internet offers unparalleled access to niche markets. Online platforms provide the tools and technologies to precisely target specific audiences that align with your product or service. By identifying and catering to these niche markets, entrepreneurs can create tailored offerings that resonate deeply with their target audience. This level of personalization fosters strong customer connections and brand loyalty, driving sustainable growth and profitability.

The online business landscape is a tapestry of diverse models and approaches, each with its own unique opportunities and challenges. E-commerce, digital services, affiliate marketing, and content creation are just a few examples of the thriving online business models available. Understanding the intricacies of these models and selecting the one that aligns with your goals and strengths is crucial for success.

Yet, while the online business landscape is ripe with opportunities, it is also fiercely competitive. To stand out amidst the digital noise, entrepreneurs must employ strategic thinking and a deep understanding of their industry and target market. Rigorous market research, competitor analysis, and consumer insights are essential for identifying gaps and opportunities, enabling businesses to craft differentiated value propositions that capture the attention and loyalty of their customers.

Building trust and credibility in the online space is paramount. As customers navigate the vast digital landscape, they seek reliability and transparency from the businesses they engage with. By establishing a strong online presence, delivering exceptional customer experiences, and cultivating authentic connections, entrepreneurs can instill confidence in their brand and foster long-term customer relationships that withstand the test of time.

In conclusion, the online business landscape represents an unparalleled realm of possibilities for ambitious entrepreneurs. The power of the internet has reshaped the business landscape, allowing individuals and small businesses to compete with established giants on a global stage. By embracing the agility, scalability, and personalization that online business offers, entrepreneurs can unlock their full potential and embark on an exhilarating journey towards entrepreneurial success. So, fasten your seatbelt and prepare to navigate the exciting twists and turns of the online business landscape – a world of boundless opportunities awaits those who dare to seize them.

_____

_____

_____

_____

_____

_____

_____

_____

_____

_____

_____

_____

_____

_____

_____

The Online Entrepreneur:
Your Comprehensive Guide to Building a Successful Business Online

CHAPTER 2:

IDENTIFYING YOUR NICHE AND TARGET MARKET

In this pivotal chapter, we delve into the essential process of identifying your niche market and understanding your target audience. Success in the online business world hinges on the ability to pinpoint a specific market segment and cater to their unique needs and preferences. By effectively defining your niche and understanding your target market, you can create a solid foundation for your online business.

To begin, thorough market research is paramount. This involves analyzing industry trends, studying competitors, and identifying gaps or underserved areas in the market. By gaining a comprehensive understanding of the competitive landscape and consumer behaviors, you can uncover opportunities and position your business strategically. Once you have identified potential market segments, it is crucial to evaluate their viability and potential profitability. Consider factors such as the size of the market, growth potential, and the level of competition. Look for segments that align with your passion, expertise, and values, as this will fuel your motivation and commitment to serving that market.

With a potential market segment in mind, the next step is to define your target audience. Develop detailed buyer personas that encapsulate the characteristics, preferences, and needs of your ideal customers. Consider factors such as demographics, psychographics, and purchasing behaviors. By creating a vivid picture of your target audience, you can tailor your marketing messages and offerings to resonate deeply with them.

In addition to demographic and psychographic information, it is crucial to understand your target audience's pain points and aspirations. What challenges do they face, and how can your product or service provide a solution? By addressing these pain points and aligning your offerings with their desires and aspirations, you can establish a strong value proposition that differentiates you from competitors.

Furthermore, conducting customer surveys or interviews can provide invaluable insights into your target audience's preferences and behaviors. This primary research can uncover hidden opportunities and help you refine your offerings to better meet their needs. Leverage digital tools and platforms to gather feedback and engage in conversations with your target audience.

As you narrow down your niche and define your target market, remember that effective communication and messaging are critical. Craft a compelling brand story and value proposition that resonates with your audience's aspirations and values. Clearly articulate the benefits and unique selling points of your products or services, highlighting how they address specific pain points or enhance the lives of your target customers.

Throughout the process, it is essential to remain agile and open to refining your niche and target market based on feedback and market dynamics. The online business landscape is ever-evolving, and being responsive to changes will enable you to stay ahead of the curve and maintain relevance in the face of shifting consumer demands.

In conclusion, identifying your niche and target market is the foundation upon which your online business will be built. Thorough market research, defining buyer personas, understanding pain points, and developing a strong value proposition are all vital components of this process. By honing in on a specific market segment and catering to their needs, you can position your online business for success. In the chapters ahead, we will delve into strategies for building your online presence, crafting effective marketing campaigns, and delivering exceptional customer experiences to solidify your position in the market. Get ready to unlock the full potential of your online business by understanding and serving your niche market with precision and dedication.

_____

_____

_____

_____

_____

_____

_____

_____

_____

_____

_____

_____

_____

_____

_____

_____

CHAPTER 3:

BUILDING YOUR ONLINE PRESENCE

In this pivotal chapter, we delve into the crucial task of building a compelling and influential online presence for your business. In today's digital age, establishing a strong and engaging online presence is essential for capturing the attention of your target audience, building brand loyalty, and driving business growth. By effectively leveraging various digital platforms and strategies, you can create a powerful online presence that sets you apart from the competition and resonates deeply with your customers.

1. *Crafting Your Brand Identity*: Your brand identity is the essence of your business, reflecting its mission, values, and unique selling proposition. Define your brand's core attributes and personality. Develop a captivating brand story that connects emotionally with your target audience, making your business more relatable and memorable. Consistency in branding across all touchpoints helps establish brand recognition and builds trust with your customers.

2. *Building a User-Centric Website*: Your website is the virtual storefront of your business, and it must captivate visitors and provide a seamless user experience. Focus on responsive web design, ensuring that your site is optimized for all devices, including desktops, tablets, and mobile phones. Incorporate intuitive navigation, engaging visuals, compelling copy, and clear calls-to-action. User-friendly features such as live chat, search

functionality, and personalized recommendations enhance the user experience and encourage conversions.

3. *Content Marketing*: Content marketing is a powerful tool for attracting, engaging, and nurturing your target audience. Develop a content strategy that aligns with your brand's values and objectives. Create high-quality and valuable content in various formats, such as blog posts, articles, videos, podcasts, and infographics. By providing relevant and insightful content, you position yourself as an authoritative resource in your industry, establish credibility, and foster long-term relationships with your audience.

4. *Search Engine Optimization (SEO)*: Optimizing your website for search engines is crucial for driving organic traffic and increasing visibility in search results. Conduct comprehensive keyword research to identify relevant and high-impact keywords. Incorporate these keywords strategically into your website's content, meta tags, headings, and URLs. Build high-quality backlinks from reputable websites to improve your search engine rankings and attract more organic traffic.

5. *Social Media Engagement*: Social media platforms offer vast opportunities for building brand awareness, engaging with your audience, and driving traffic to your website. Identify the social media platforms that align with your target audience's preferences and behavior. Develop a content strategy that encourages conversation, educates, entertains, and inspires your audience. Actively engage with your followers, respond to comments and messages promptly, and foster a sense of community through contests, polls, and user-generated content.

6. *Email Marketing*: Building an email list allows you to establish direct communication with your audience and nurture relationships over time. Create compelling opt-in incentives to encourage visitors to subscribe to your email list. Design and send regular newsletters that provide valuable content, updates,

and exclusive offers. Personalize your emails based on subscriber preferences and behaviors, segmenting your audience to deliver targeted and relevant messaging that resonates with their needs and interests.

7. *Online Advertising*: Strategic online advertising can drive targeted traffic to your website and boost brand visibility. Explore paid advertising options such as search engine marketing (SEM), display advertising, and social media advertising. Define clear objectives for your campaigns, identify your target audience, and craft compelling ad copies that align with their needs and motivations. Monitor and optimize your campaigns regularly to maximize their effectiveness and return on investment.

8. *User Experience (UX) Design*: Providing a seamless and enjoyable user experience is critical for attracting and retaining website visitors. Optimize your website's loading speed, ensure intuitive navigation, and streamline the checkout process to minimize friction. Conduct usability testing and analyze user behavior to uncover opportunities for improvement. Continuously iterate and refine your website's design and functionality to enhance user satisfaction and drive conversions.

9. *Data Analytics and Insights*: Implementing robust analytics tools allows you to gather and analyze data to gain valuable insights into your online presence's performance. Track and measure key metrics such as website traffic, user engagement, conversion rates, and customer acquisition costs. Leverage data-driven insights to make informed decisions and optimize your online presence continually. Monitor market trends, consumer behavior, and emerging technologies to stay ahead of the competition and adapt your strategies accordingly.

10. *Online Reputation Management*: Managing your online reputation is crucial for building trust and credibility with your audience. Monitor online reviews, social media mentions, and customer feedback to stay aware of your brand's perception. Respond

promptly and professionally to both positive and negative feedback, demonstrating your commitment to customer satisfaction and problem resolution. Encourage and facilitate positive customer reviews to enhance your online reputation and attract new customers.

By focusing on these critical aspects of building your online presence, you can establish a captivating and influential digital footprint that attracts, engages, and retains customers. Building an online presence is an ongoing process that requires continuous effort, adaptability, and innovation. In the chapters ahead, we will explore strategies for developing a winning business strategy, driving online sales, and fostering lasting customer relationships. Get ready to elevate your online presence to new heights and make a lasting impact in the digital landscape.

_____

_____

_____

_____

_____

_____

_____

_____

_____

_____

_____

_____

_____

_____

_____

_____

_____

_____

The Online Entrepreneur:
Your Comprehensive Guide to Building a Successful Business Online

CHAPTER 4:

DEVELOPING A WINNING BUSINESS STRATEGY

In this critical chapter, we explore the essential elements of developing a winning business strategy for your online venture. A well-crafted and comprehensive strategy is the roadmap that guides your business towards success, helping you navigate challenges, make informed decisions, and achieve your goals. By focusing on key areas such as goal-setting, planning, and implementation, you can lay a solid foundation for sustained growth and profitability.

1. *Setting Clear Business Goals*: Define clear and measurable goals that align with your overall vision for the business. Whether it's revenue targets, customer acquisition goals, or market share objectives, setting specific and achievable goals provides a sense of direction and purpose. Ensure your goals are realistic, time-bound, and aligned with the needs and expectations of your target audience.

2. *Conducting a SWOT Analysis*: Performing a comprehensive SWOT (Strengths, Weaknesses, Opportunities, Threats) analysis allows you to assess the internal and external factors that impact your business. Identify your strengths and leverage them to gain a competitive advantage. Recognize weaknesses and develop strategies to overcome them. Explore opportunities in the market and anticipate potential threats. A thorough analysis

provides valuable insights that shape your strategic decisions.

3. *Crafting a Comprehensive Business Plan*: Developing a detailed business plan is crucial for mapping out your path to success. It should encompass your mission, vision, target market, competitive analysis, marketing and sales strategies, operational plans, and financial projections. A well-structured business plan serves as a blueprint for your business's operations and growth, guiding you through various stages and ensuring that you stay focused and on track.

4. *Implementing Effective Sales Funnels*: Designing and implementing effective sales funnels is vital for converting leads into paying customers. Understand the different stages of the customer journey, from awareness to consideration and decision-making. Develop strategies and tactics for each stage to nurture leads, build trust, and ultimately drive conversions. Employ marketing automation tools and personalized messaging to streamline the process and maximize sales potential.

5. *Customer Acquisition Strategies*: Develop targeted customer acquisition strategies to expand your customer base. Utilize a mix of online marketing channels such as search engine marketing (SEM), social media advertising, content marketing, and influencer partnerships. Tailor your messaging and promotions to resonate with your target audience's needs and motivations. Continually analyze and optimize your customer acquisition efforts based on data and performance metrics.

6. *Building Customer Relationships*: Fostering strong and lasting relationships with your customers is critical for long-term success. Implement customer relationship management (CRM) systems to track customer interactions, preferences, and purchase history. Personalize your communications and provide exceptional customer service at every touchpoint. Encourage customer feedback and actively seek ways to enhance the customer experience. Repeat customers and brand advocates are

invaluable assets for sustainable growth.

7. *Innovation and Adaptation*: In the rapidly evolving digital landscape, innovation and adaptability are key to staying ahead of the competition. Continuously monitor industry trends, technological advancements, and customer preferences. Embrace emerging technologies that can enhance your operations and deliver new value to your customers. Foster a culture of creativity and encourage employees to contribute ideas for innovation and improvement.

8. *Financial Planning and Budgeting*: Develop a robust financial plan that includes revenue forecasts, expense budgets, and cash flow projections. Regularly review and analyze financial performance to ensure the business remains on track. Implement effective cost management strategies and monitor key financial metrics to make informed decisions. Consider seeking professional advice from accountants or financial advisors to optimize your financial planning.

9. *Risk Management*: Identify and assess potential risks that could impact your business. Develop strategies to mitigate these risks and ensure business continuity. This may involve contingency plans, insurance coverage, or diversification strategies. Stay informed about legal and regulatory requirements to maintain compliance and avoid potential pitfalls.

10. *Monitoring and Evaluation*: Regularly monitor and evaluate key performance indicators (KPIs) to gauge the effectiveness of your business strategy. This includes metrics such as revenue growth, customer acquisition costs, customer retention rates, and website analytics. Utilize data-driven insights to identify areas for improvement, make informed decisions, and refine your business strategy accordingly.

By focusing on these crucial aspects of developing a winning business strategy, you can position your online venture for long-term success. A well-defined strategy provides clarity, direction, and a solid framework for growth. In the chapters ahead, we will explore specific tactics and tools to implement your strategy effectively and achieve your business objectives. Get ready to chart your course towards success with a robust and dynamic business strategy that sets you apart in the competitive online landscape.

Risk management: Safeguarding your online business

In today's dynamic and unpredictable business landscape, effective risk management is paramount for the long-term success and sustainability of your online business. By proactively identifying potential risks and implementing strategies to mitigate them, you can protect your business from unforeseen events and maintain a competitive edge. In this section, we will delve deeper into the essential components of risk management and highlight key practices to safeguard your online venture.

1. *Identify Potential Risks*: Begin by conducting a thorough assessment to identify potential risks specific to your online business. This may include cybersecurity threats, data breaches, legal and regulatory compliance issues, operational disruptions, market volatility, or reputational risks. By understanding the potential risks, you can take proactive measures to minimize their impact.

2. *Evaluate Risk Impact and Probability*: Assess the potential impact and probability of each identified risk. Consider the potential financial, operational, and reputational consequences of each risk event. Evaluate the likelihood of each risk occurring, taking, into account historical data, industry trends, and expert opinions. This evaluation will help prioritize your risk management efforts and allocate resources effectively.

3. *Develop Risk Mitigation Strategies*: Once risks are identified and evaluated, develop comprehensive risk mitigation strategies to minimize the likelihood and impact of potential risks. This may

involve implementing robust cybersecurity measures, establishing data protection protocols, ensuring legal and regulatory compliance, and implementing backup and disaster recovery plans. Consider investing in insurance coverage tailored to your specific industry and business needs.

4. *Continuously Monitor and Update Risk Management Strategies*: Risk management is an ongoing process that requires continuous monitoring and adjustment. Stay informed about emerging risks, technological advancements, and changes in the regulatory landscape. Regularly reassess the effectiveness of your risk management strategies and update them as necessary. Implement a culture of risk awareness within your organization and provide training to employees to ensure everyone understands their roles and responsibilities in managing risks.

5. *Develop a Business Continuity Plan*: Create a comprehensive business continuity plan that outlines procedures to be followed in the event of a major risk event or business disruption. This plan should include steps to restore critical operations, communication protocols, alternative suppliers, and employee safety measures. Regularly test and update the plan to ensure its effectiveness and readiness.

6. *Maintain Secure Data Management*: Data security is of utmost importance in the online business realm. Implement robust data protection measures, including secure encryption, regular data backups, access controls, and employee training on data handling best practices. Stay informed about data privacy regulations and ensure compliance to build trust with your customers and protect sensitive information.

7. *Establish Strategic Partnerships*: Collaborating with trusted partners can help mitigate certain risks and enhance your business resilience. Establish partnerships with reliable vendors, suppliers, and service providers who adhere to high security standards and have strong contingency plans in place. Regularly

assess and monitor the performance of your partners to ensure they meet your risk management requirements.

8. *Maintain Legal and Regulatory Compliance*: Stay up to date with applicable laws, regulations, and industry standards related to your online business. Regularly review and assess your compliance status, ensuring adherence to data protection regulations, consumer protection laws, intellectual property rights, and other relevant legal requirements. Consult legal experts to ensure your business practices align with the evolving legal landscape.

9. *Conduct Periodic Risk Assessments*: Perform regular risk assessments to identify new and emerging risks that may impact your online business. Consider changes in the business environment, technological advancements, market trends, and customer preferences. By staying vigilant and proactive in identifying potential risks, you can adapt your risk management strategies and maintain a competitive advantage.

10. *Seek Professional Advice*: Risk management can be complex, and seeking professional advice from risk management specialists or consultants can provide valuable insights and expertise. They can help identify potential blind spots, assess risk exposures, and recommend tailored risk management solutions that align with your business objectives.

By implementing robust risk management practices, you can protect your online business from potential threats and ensure its long-term viability. Prioritize risk management as an integral part of your business strategy, and continuously monitor and adapt your risk mitigation efforts. By doing so, you can navigate uncertainties with confidence and position your online business for sustained success in an ever-changing business landscape.

_____

_____

_____

_____

_____

_____

_____

_____

_____

_____

_____

_____

_____

_____

_____

_____

The Online Entrepreneur:
Your Comprehensive Guide to Building a Successful Business Online

CHAPTER 5:

DRIVING ONLINE SALES

In this pivotal chapter, we explore the strategies and tactics necessary to drive online sales and maximize revenue for your business. As an online entrepreneur, your success depends on your ability to attract and convert customers in the digital marketplace. By focusing on key areas such as lead generation, conversion optimization, and customer retention, you can build a strong foundation for sustainable growth and profitability.

5.1 Lead Generation

In this section, we will delve into effective lead generation strategies to attract potential customers and expand your customer base.

1. *Targeted Marketing Campaigns:* Craft targeted marketing campaigns to reach your ideal customer demographic. Utilize data and market research to understand their needs, preferences, and pain points. Tailor your messaging and promotions to resonate with their interests and motivations. Employ a mix of digital marketing channels, such as search engine marketing (SEM), social media advertising, content marketing, and email marketing, to amplify your reach.

2. *Compelling Landing Pages:* Create compelling landing pages that

engage visitors and entice them to take action. Optimize your landing pages with persuasive copy, clear calls-to-action, and compelling visuals. A/B test different elements to optimize conversion rates. Capture leads through forms and provide valuable incentives, such as eBooks, whitepapers, or exclusive discounts, in exchange for contact information.

3. *Content Marketing*: Develop high-quality, informative, and shareable content that attracts and engages your target audience. Publish blog posts, articles, videos, or podcasts that address their pain points, offer solutions, and establish your authority in the industry. Optimize content for search engines to increase organic traffic and attract qualified leads.

4. *Social Media Engagement*: Leverage social media platforms to engage with your audience and build brand awareness. Create compelling and shareable content that encourages likes, comments, and shares. Actively respond to comments, messages, and mentions to foster connections and drive engagement. Utilize social media advertising to target specific segments of your audience and drive lead generation.

5.2: Conversion Optimization

In this section, we will focus on strategies to optimize conversions and turn leads into paying customers.

1. *User-Friendly Website Design*: Ensure your website is user-friendly and optimized for conversions. Streamline the navigation, eliminate clutter, and make the checkout process seamless. Optimize page loading speed and ensure responsive design for mobile devices. Conduct user testing to identify any barriers to conversion and make necessary improvements.

2. *Compelling Product Descriptions and Visuals*: Create persuasive product descriptions that highlight the features, benefits, and unique selling points of your offerings. Utilize high-quality

images, videos, and 360-degree views to showcase products from different angles. Incorporate customer reviews and testimonials to build trust and credibility.

3. *Simplified Checkout Process*: Minimize friction in the checkout process to reduce cart abandonment rates. Implement a streamlined and user-friendly checkout flow, allowing for guest checkouts and providing multiple payment options. Clearly communicate shipping costs, return policies, and estimated delivery times to enhance transparency and alleviate customer concerns.

4. *Personalization and Recommendations*: Implement personalization techniques to enhance the customer experience and drive conversions. Utilize customer data to provide personalized recommendations based on browsing and purchase history. Implement dynamic pricing or discounts based on customer segments or behaviors. Leverage upselling and cross-selling opportunities to increase average order value.

5.3: Customer Retention

In this section, we will explore strategies to nurture customer relationships and drive repeat purchases.

1. *Exceptional Customer Service*: Provide outstanding customer service at every touchpoint. Respond promptly to inquiries and resolve issues efficiently. Personalize interactions to make customers feel valued and appreciated. Implement self-service options, such as FAQs or chatbots, to provide immediate assistance.

2. *Loyalty Programs*: Implement a customer loyalty program to incentivize repeat purchases and reward customer loyalty. Offer exclusive discounts, early access to new products, or special perks for loyal customers. Encourage referrals by providing incentives for customers who refer friends or family members.

3. *Email Marketing Campaigns*: Develop targeted email marketing campaigns to engage and nurture existing customers. Segment your email list based on customer preferences, behaviors, or purchase history. Provide personalized product recommendations, exclusive offers, and relevant content. Send regular newsletters to keep customers informed and engaged.

4. *Social Media Community Building*: Foster a sense of community and brand advocacy through social media. Encourage customers to share their experiences, testimonials, or user-generated content. Engage with followers by responding to comments, running contests or giveaways, and sharing relevant content. Implement social listening strategies to monitor and address customer feedback.

By implementing these strategies for driving online sales, you can maximize revenue and build a loyal customer base. Continually evaluate and refine your tactics based on data and customer insights. In the chapters ahead, we will explore additional methods to enhance your marketing efforts, optimize your operations, and grow your online business to new heights of success. Get ready to unleash your sales potential and thrive in the ever-evolving digital marketplace.

_____

_____

_____

_____

_____

_____

_____

_____

_____

_____

_____

_____

_____

_____

_____

_____

CHAPTER 6:

DELIVERING EXCEPTIONAL CUSTOMER EXPERIENCES

Now we'll dive into the critical importance of delivering exceptional customer experiences in the online business world. The satisfaction and loyalty of your customers directly impact the success and growth of your business. By focusing on key areas such as customer service, personalization, post-purchase support, and continuous improvement, you can build strong customer relationships and differentiate your online business from the competition.

6.1: Customer Service Excellence

In this section, we explore the strategies and practices to deliver exceptional customer service.

1. *Prompt and Responsive Communication*: Respond to customer inquiries, messages, and concerns promptly and professionally. Provide multiple communication channels such as email, live chat, and phone support to accommodate customer preferences. Set clear response time expectations and strive to exceed them.

2. *Empathy and Understanding*: Practice empathy when interacting with customers. Listen actively, understand their needs, and demonstrate genuine concern for their issues. Train your

customer service team to handle challenging situations with empathy and professionalism.

3. *Knowledgeable Support Staff:* Equip your customer service team with the necessary knowledge and tools to address customer queries effectively. Provide comprehensive training on your products or services, policies, and common issues. Foster a culture of continuous learning and ensure that your team stays up to date with industry trends.

4. *Customer Feedback and Satisfaction Surveys:* Implement mechanisms to gather customer feedback and measure satisfaction levels. Encourage customers to provide feedback through surveys, reviews, or testimonials. Regularly analyze and act upon the feedback received to improve your products, services, and customer experiences.

6.2: Personalization and Customization

In this section, we explore the benefits of personalization and customization in creating memorable customer experiences.

1. *Personalized Recommendations:* Utilize customer data and purchase history to provide personalized product recommendations. Use browsing behavior and demographic information to deliver targeted offers or content that align with their preferences and interests. Leverage technology such as machine learning algorithms to enhance personalization efforts.

2. *Tailored Marketing Messages:* Craft targeted marketing messages that resonate with individual customers. Segment your customer base based on demographics, purchasing behavior, or interests. Tailor your email marketing campaigns, social media content, and advertising to deliver relevant messages that capture their attention.

3. *Customization Options:* Offer customization options to allow customers to personalize products or services to their specific

needs and preferences. Enable them to select colors, sizes, features, or add-ons that suit their preferences. Provide a seamless and user-friendly customization process to enhance the overall customer experience.

6.3: Post-Purchase Support and Engagement

In this section, we explore the importance of post-purchase support and ongoing engagement with customers.

1. *Order Tracking and Delivery Updates*: Keep customers informed about the status of their orders through order tracking systems and regular delivery updates. Provide estimated delivery times and courier information. Address any delivery issues promptly to ensure a smooth and reliable post-purchase experience.

2. *Proactive Support and Follow-Up*: Reach out to customers after their purchase to ensure their satisfaction and address any potential issues. Proactively seek feedback on their experience and provide assistance or guidance if needed. Demonstrate your commitment to their satisfaction and willingness to resolve any concerns.

3. *Loyalty Programs and Rewards*: Implement loyalty programs to reward customers for their repeat business. Offer incentives such as exclusive discounts, early access to new products, or special promotions. Engage with loyal customers through personalized communications and express gratitude for their ongoing support.

6.4: Continuous Improvement and Innovation

In this section, we emphasize the importance of continuous

improvement and innovation in delivering exceptional customer experiences.

1. *Customer Journey Mapping*: Map out the customer journey to identify touchpoints, pain points, and areas for improvement. Gain insights into the customer's experience from initial engagement to post-purchase interactions. Use this information to streamline processes, reduce friction, and enhance the overall customer journey.

2. *Data Analytics and Insights*: Leverage data analytics tools to gain insights into customer behaviors, preferences, and trends. Analyze customer interactions, purchase patterns, and engagement metrics to identify areas for optimization. Use data-driven insights to make informed decisions and enhance customer experiences.

3. *Technology and Automation*: Leverage technology and automation to streamline processes and enhance customer experiences. Implement chatbots or virtual assistants to provide immediate support and answers to frequently asked questions. Use customer relationship management (CRM) systems to track customer interactions, preferences, and purchase history.

4. *Feedback Utilization*: Actively listen to customer feedback and use it to drive improvements. Regularly analyze feedback data to identify trends, recurring issues, or areas for enhancement. Implement changes based on customer feedback to continually improve your products, services, and overall customer experience.

By focusing on delivering exceptional customer experiences, you can foster customer loyalty, drive positive word-of-mouth, and differentiate your online business from competitors. Continually evaluate and refine your strategies based on customer feedback, emerging trends, and technological advancements. In the chapters ahead, we will explore additional techniques to optimize your operations, nurture customer relationships, and drive sustainable growth in the online business landscape. Prepare to elevate your customer experiences and create lasting connections with your target audience.

The Online Entrepreneur:
Your Comprehensive Guide to Building a Successful Business Online

The Online Entrepreneur:
Your Comprehensive Guide to Building a Successful Business Online

CHAPTER 7:

OPTIMIZING OPERATIONS AND EFFICIENCY

In this pivotal chapter, we delve into the strategies and practices for optimizing operations and improving efficiency in your online business. By streamlining processes, leveraging technology, and implementing effective management techniques, you can enhance productivity, reduce costs, and drive overall business performance.

7.1: Streamlining Processes

In this section, we explore strategies to streamline your business processes and eliminate unnecessary inefficiencies.

1. *Process Mapping and Analysis*: Let's consider the process of order fulfillment in an e-commerce business. Map out each step involved, from order processing and inventory management to shipping and delivery. Identify areas where delays or bottlenecks occur, and implement measures to streamline the process, such as automating order notifications to the warehouse for faster picking and packing.

2. *Standard Operating Procedures (SOPs)*: Develop standardized procedures for customer returns and exchanges. Create an SOP that outlines the steps to be followed, including how to handle return requests, issue refunds, or process exchanges. By

establishing clear and consistent procedures, you can ensure that returns are handled efficiently and customers receive timely resolution.

3. *Automation and Workflow Tools*: For example, leverage automation tools to streamline repetitive tasks, such as email marketing campaigns. Use an email marketing platform that allows you to create automated workflows based on triggers and customer behavior. Set up workflows to send personalized emails, such as welcome emails to new subscribers or abandoned cart reminders with tailored offers.

4. *Outsourcing and Delegation*: Consider outsourcing customer support to a specialized contact center. By partnering with a professional team, you can ensure that customer inquiries and issues are handled promptly and effectively, freeing up your internal resources to focus on core business activities like product development or marketing.

7.2: Technology Integration

In this section, we discuss the importance of integrating technology into your operations for improved efficiency.

1. *Cloud Computing and Data Management*: Utilize cloud-based storage and collaboration tools to centralize your business data and facilitate real-time access for your team. This allows team members to collaborate seamlessly, even when working remotely, and eliminates the need for manual file sharing or version control.

2. *Customer Relationship Management (CRM) Systems*: For instance, implement a CRM system to consolidate customer data, track interactions, and manage sales pipelines. Use the CRM to automate lead nurturing, track customer communications, and generate insightful reports. This enables you to effectively manage customer relationships and personalize marketing

efforts.

3. *Inventory and Supply Chain Management*: Integrate an inventory management system with your e-commerce platform to optimize inventory levels and automate replenishment. Set up alerts for low stock levels and establish reorder points to ensure you never run out of popular products. By automating inventory management, you can minimize stockouts and overstock situations.

4. *Analytics and Reporting*: Utilize web analytics tools to monitor website performance and customer behavior. Track metrics such as website traffic, conversion rates, and customer engagement. Use these insights to identify areas for improvement, such as optimizing landing pages, refining marketing campaigns, or enhancing user experience.

7.3: Effective Team Management

In this section, we focus on techniques for managing your team effectively and fostering a culture of productivity.

1. *Clear Roles and Responsibilities*: Clearly define roles and responsibilities within your team, outlining who is responsible for specific tasks or areas of expertise. This clarity ensures that everyone understands their responsibilities and avoids confusion or duplication of efforts.

2. *Training and Development*: Invest in ongoing training and development programs to enhance your team's skills and knowledge. Offer opportunities for professional growth, such as attending industry conferences or providing access to online learning platforms. By continuously improving your team's capabilities, you can boost productivity and adapt to evolving business needs.

3. *Performance Measurement and Accountability*: Establish key performance indicators (KPIs) for each team member that align

with business objectives. Regularly review individual performance against these metrics and provide feedback to help them improve. Recognize and reward top performers to foster a sense of accountability and motivate your team.

4. *Effective Communication and Collaboration*: For example, leverage communication and collaboration tools to facilitate efficient information sharing and teamwork. Utilize project management platforms, chat applications, and video conferencing tools to ensure seamless communication and collaboration, regardless of team members' locations or time zones.

By optimizing operations and improving efficiency, you can streamline your business processes, enhance productivity, and drive overall business success. Continuously evaluate and refine your operations, leveraging technology, and embracing best practices. In the chapters ahead, we will explore additional strategies to scale your business, adapt to changing market dynamics, and thrive in the competitive online landscape. Get ready to optimize your operations and unlock your business's full potential.

_____

_____

_____

_____

_____

_____

_____

_____

_____

_____

_____

_____

_____

_____

_____

_____

CHAPTER 8:

SCALING YOUR ONLINE BUSINESS

In this chapter, we explore the strategies and considerations for scaling your online business to new heights. Scaling involves increasing your customer base, and maximizing your revenue while maintaining efficiency and profitability. By focusing on key areas such as market research, customer acquisition, and strategic partnerships, you can position your business for long-term growth and success.

8.1: Market Research and Analysis

In this section, we discuss the importance of conducting thorough market research and analysis before scaling your online business.

1. *Target Market Identification:* Identify your target market by analyzing demographics, psychographics, and consumer behaviors. Understand their needs, preferences, and pain points. Use tools such as customer surveys, market research reports, and competitor analysis to gather insights.

2. *Competitive Analysis:* Study your competitors' strengths, weaknesses, and market positioning. Identify gaps in the market and areas where your business can differentiate itself. This analysis can help you develop unique value propositions and competitive advantages.

3. *Market Trends and Opportunities*: Stay informed about industry trends, emerging technologies, and shifts in consumer behavior. Identify opportunities for innovation and anticipate future market demands. This knowledge can guide your product development, marketing strategies, and overall business direction.

8.2: Customer Acquisition and Retention

In this section, we explore strategies for acquiring new customers and retaining existing ones as you scale your online business.

1. *Scalable Marketing Channels*: Leverage digital marketing channels such as search engine optimization (SEO), social media advertising, influencer partnerships, and content marketing. These channels allow you to reach a wider audience and drive targeted traffic to your website or online store.

2. *Customer Relationship Management*: Implement a robust customer relationship management (CRM) system to manage customer interactions and nurture relationships. Utilize personalized email marketing campaigns, loyalty programs, and customer feedback initiatives to strengthen customer loyalty and drive repeat purchases.

3. *Exceptional Customer Service*: Prioritize exceptional customer service as you scale your business. Train your customer support team to provide timely and personalized assistance. Implement self-service options, such as detailed FAQs or chatbots, to address common inquiries and provide 24/7 support.

8.3: Operational Scalability

In this section, we discuss strategies for scaling your business operations to handle increased demand and maintain efficiency.

1. *Scalable Infrastructure*: Asses your current infrastructure and

determine if it can accommodate future growth. Invest in scalable hosting solutions, cloud-based storage, and reliable website hosting to handle increased traffic and ensure a seamless user experience.

2. *Process Automation*: Automate repetitive tasks and streamline workflows using software solutions. Implement order management systems, inventory management tools, and automated customer support platforms to reduce manual workload and improve operational efficiency.

3. *Supply Chain Management*: Establish strong relationships with suppliers and distributors to ensure a reliable supply chain. Negotiate favorable terms, maintain adequate inventory levels, and explore outsourcing options to handle increased production or fulfillment demands.

8.4: Strategic Partnerships

In this section, we explore the benefits of forming strategic partnerships to support your business growth.

1. *Collaborative Marketing Efforts*: Collaborate with complementary businesses or influencers to expand your reach and tap into new customer segments. Co-create content, run joint marketing campaigns, or offer bundled products or services to leverage each other's audiences.

2. *Supplier and Vendor Partnerships*: Develop strategic partnerships with reliable suppliers or vendors to ensure consistent product quality and availability. Negotiate favorable pricing, secure exclusive deals, or explore drop shipping options to reduce inventory risks.

3. *Distribution and Fulfillment Partnerships*: For instance, partner with third-party logistics (3PL) providers or fulfillment centers to handle increased order volume and shipping demands. This allows you to focus on core business activities while ensuring

efficient order fulfillment and timely delivery.

8.5: Financial Management and Planning

In this section, we delve into the importance of effective financial management and planning as you scale your online business.

1. *Budgeting and Forecasting*: Create a comprehensive budget that outlines your expected revenue, expenses, and investments for the scaling phase. Use financial forecasting techniques to project future cash flows and make informed decisions regarding resource allocation and business growth.

2. *Cost Optimization*: Analyze your cost structure and identify areas where you can optimize expenses without compromising quality. Negotiate favorable terms with suppliers, explore cost-saving measures in operations, and leverage technology to automate processes and reduce overhead costs.

3. *Financial Performance Tracking*: For example, establish key financial metrics and performance indicators to monitor the financial health of your business. Regularly track revenue, profit margins, customer acquisition costs, and other financial metrics. Utilize accounting software or engage professional accountants to ensure accurate and up-to-date financial records.

8.6: Monitoring and Evaluation

In this section, we discuss the importance of monitoring and evaluating your scaling efforts to make informed decisions and drive continuous improvement.

1. *Performance Reviews and Analysis*: For example, conduct regular performance reviews to assess the effectiveness of your scaling strategies. Analyze the impact of your initiatives on key business metrics and make data-driven decisions. Identify successful tactics and areas that require adjustment or further investment.

2. *Customer Feedback and Satisfaction*: Actively seek feedback from your customers to gauge their satisfaction levels and identify areas for improvement. Utilize surveys, reviews, or customer support interactions to gather insights. Leverage customer feedback to enhance your products, services, and overall customer experience.

3. *Continuous Improvement Initiatives*: For instance, foster a culture of continuous improvement by encouraging innovation and embracing feedback. Encourage your team to propose ideas for process optimization, product enhancements, or customer experience improvements. Regularly assess and prioritize these initiatives to drive ongoing growth and customer satisfaction.

By focusing on market research, customer acquisition and retention, operational scalability, and strategic partnerships, you can successfully scale your online business. Continuously evaluate market trends, adapt your strategies, and refine your operations to meet the evolving needs of your target audience. In the chapters ahead, we will explore additional strategies for sustainability, innovation, and long-term success in the dynamic world of online business. Prepare to take your business to new heights and achieve remarkable growth.

_____

_____

_____

_____

_____

_____

_____

_____

_____

_____

_____

_____

_____

_____

_____

_____

_____

_____

_____

_____

_____

_____

_____

_____

_____

_____

_____

_____

_____

_____

_____

_____

The Online Entrepreneur:
Your Comprehensive Guide to Building a Successful Business Online

CHAPTER 9:

INNOVATION AND ADAPTATION

In this transformative chapter, we delve into the importance of innovation and adaptation in the ever-evolving online business landscape. By fostering a culture of innovation, embracing emerging technologies, and staying attuned to customer needs, you can drive continuous growth, remain competitive, and seize new opportunities.

9.1: Cultivating a Culture of Innovation

In this section, we explore strategies for fostering a culture of innovation within your online business.

1. *Encouraging Idea Generation*: Create platforms or channels for employees to share their ideas and suggestions. Implement regular brainstorming sessions or innovation workshops to spark creativity and generate innovative solutions. Foster an open and inclusive environment where ideas are valued and encouraged.

2. *Embracing Experimentation*: Allocate resources and time for experimentation and pilot projects. Encourage your team to test new ideas, products, or marketing strategies. Embrace a fail-fast mentality that values learning from setbacks and using insights gained to drive future innovation.

3. *Collaboration and Cross-Functional Teams*: Encourage cross-

functional collaboration by bringing together individuals from different departments or areas of expertise to work on specific projects. This collaboration fosters diverse perspectives, sparks creativity, and promotes innovative thinking.

4. *Continuous Learning and Development*: Invest in ongoing learning and development opportunities for your team. Offer training programs, workshops, or access to online resources that keep them updated on industry trends, emerging technologies, and innovative practices. Encourage a growth mindset and a passion for learning.

9.2: Embracing Emerging Technologies

In this section, we discuss the importance of embracing emerging technologies to drive innovation and improve business operations.

1. *Artificial Intelligence (AI) and Machine Learning*: Leverage AI and machine learning algorithms to analyze customer data, predict buying patterns, and personalize customer experiences. Implement chatbots or virtual assistants to enhance customer support and automate repetitive tasks.

2. *Internet of Things (IoT)*: Explore opportunities to integrate IoT devices and sensors into your products or business operations. This can enable real-time monitoring, remote management, and the collection of valuable data for better decision-making and process optimization.

3. *Big Data Analytics*: Harness the power of big data by implementing advanced analytics tools. Analyze large datasets to gain insights into customer behavior, market trends, and operational efficiency. Use these insights to drive informed decision-making and identify new business opportunities.

4. *Blockchain Technology*: Consider leveraging blockchain technology to enhance transparency, security, and trust in your business processes. Explore applications such as supply chain

management, digital identity verification, or smart contracts that streamline transactions and reduce intermediaries.

9.3: Customer-Centric Innovation

In this section, we explore the importance of customer-centric innovation and understanding customer needs.

1. *Customer Research and Insights*: Conduct regular market research, customer surveys, and focus groups to gain a deep understanding of your target audience's needs, preferences, and pain points. Use these insights to drive product development, service enhancements, and overall customer experience improvements.

2. *Co-Creation and Feedback Loops*: Involve customers in the innovation process through co-creation initiatives or beta testing programs. Seek their feedback and incorporate their suggestions into product iterations or service enhancements. This collaborative approach fosters a sense of ownership and creates products that truly meet customer needs.

3. *User Experience Design*: Invest in user experience (UX) design to create intuitive and seamless digital experiences. Conduct usability testing, analyze user flows, and optimize interfaces to ensure a smooth and enjoyable customer journey. Continuously iterate and improve based on user feedback and evolving market trends.

4. *Agile Product Development*: Adopt agile methodologies in your product development process. Break down projects into smaller, iterative phases and involve cross-functional teams for rapid prototyping, testing, and iteration. This approach allows you to respond quickly to market feedback and deliver products that meet customer demands.

9.4: Collaboration and Partnerships

In this section, we explore the power of collaboration and strategic partnerships in fostering innovation and driving business growth.

1. *Industry Collaborations*: Collaborate with other businesses or organizations within your industry to exchange knowledge, share resources, and drive innovation. Join industry associations or participate in collaborative projects to tap into a collective pool of expertise and leverage shared opportunities.

2. *Academic and Research Partnerships*: Establish partnerships with academic institutions or research organizations to access cutting-edge research, insights, and technology. Collaborate on research projects, sponsor internships or scholarships, and tap into the expertise of professors or researchers to gain a competitive edge.

3. *Startup Incubators and Accelerators*: Leverage the support of startup incubators or accelerators to gain access to a network of entrepreneurs, mentors, and investors. Collaborate with startups on pilot projects or innovation challenges to foster fresh ideas and tap into their agility and entrepreneurial spirit.

4. *Supplier and Vendor Collaborations*: Collaborate closely with your suppliers or vendors to drive mutual innovation and enhance operational efficiency. Share insights, explore joint product development opportunities, or negotiate strategic partnerships that benefit both parties and create a competitive advantage.

9.5: Agile Leadership and Adaptability

In this section, we explore the role of agile leadership in driving innovation and leading your online business through change and uncertainty.

1. *Vision and Strategy Alignment*: Define a clear vision and strategy that aligns with market trends, customer expectations, and your organization's core values. Communicate this vision to your

team and empower them to contribute their ideas and insights.

2. *Empowering and Agile Team Culture*: Foster a culture of agility, flexibility, and continuous learning within your team. Encourage experimentation, embrace failure as an opportunity for growth, and empower team members to take ownership of their projects and decisions.

3. *Embracing Change and Risk-Taking*: Promote a mindset that embraces change and encourages calculated risk-taking. Encourage team members to challenge the status quo, explore new ideas, and be open to innovation. Provide a safe environment where mistakes are seen as learning opportunities.

4. *Iterative Decision-Making*: Adopt an iterative approach to decision-making, allowing for quick experiments, feedback loops, and adjustments. Break down large initiatives into smaller, manageable tasks that can be tested, measured, and refined. Iterate based on data, customer insights, and market feedback.

By cultivating a culture of innovation, embracing emerging technologies, and prioritizing customer-centric approaches, you can drive continuous growth and stay ahead in the competitive online business landscape. Continuously scan the market for new trends, listen to customer feedback, and adapt your strategies accordingly. In the chapters ahead, we will explore additional strategies for leadership, sustainability, and achieving long-term success in the dynamic world of online business. Get ready to innovate, adapt, and thrive in the digital era.

_____

_____

_____

_____

_____

_____

_____

_____

_____

_____

_____

_____

_____

_____

_____

CHAPTER 10:

OVERCOMING CHALLENGES AND EMBRACING SUCCESS

Let's dive in and discover how to overcome challenges and embrace success in your online business.

Identifying and Addressing Common Challenges:

1. *Market Saturation*: As the online business landscape becomes increasingly competitive, entrepreneurs may face challenges in standing out from the crowd. Effective strategies to overcome market saturation include niche targeting, differentiation through unique value propositions, and staying abreast of market trends.

2. *Technology Obstacles*: Online businesses rely heavily on technology, and technical challenges can impede success. Overcoming technology obstacles involves building a strong tech infrastructure, partnering with reliable service providers, and staying updated on emerging technologies.

3. *Customer Acquisition and Retention*: Acquiring and retaining customers is a continual challenge for online entrepreneurs. Strategies such as targeted marketing campaigns, personalized customer experiences, and loyalty programs can help overcome this challenge and build a strong customer base.

Cultivating a Growth Mindset:

1. *Embracing Change:* A growth mindset is crucial for overcoming challenges and embracing success. It involves viewing setbacks as opportunities for learning and growth, being open to change, and adapting to evolving market dynamics.
2. *Continuous Learning:* Successful online entrepreneurs prioritize continuous learning and skill development. This can be achieved through industry research, attending relevant workshops or conferences, and seeking mentorship or guidance from experts in the field.
3. Innovation and Adaptability: Embracing innovation and being adaptable to change are key drivers of success. Online businesses must continuously innovate their products, services, and strategies to stay ahead of the competition and meet evolving customer needs.

Celebrating Milestones and Setting New Goals:

1. *Recognizing Achievements:* Celebrating milestones along the entrepreneurial journey is important for motivation and morale. Recognize and acknowledge accomplishments, whether it's reaching a revenue target, expanding into new markets, or receiving positive customer feedback.
2. *Setting New Goals:* Success is an ongoing process, and setting new goals is essential for continued growth. Set ambitious yet achievable goals that align with your long-term vision. These goals can include expanding into new markets, launching new product lines, or increasing customer retention rates.
3. *Regular Evaluation and Reflection:* Periodically evaluate your progress and reflect on lessons learned. Analyze successes and failures, gather feedback from customers and team members,

and adjust strategies accordingly to maintain a forward trajectory.

Overcoming challenges and embracing success in the online business world requires a combination of strategic thinking, adaptability, and continuous growth. By identifying and addressing common challenges, cultivating a growth mindset, and celebrating milestones while setting new goals, entrepreneurs can overcome obstacles and propel their online businesses to new heights of success. Remember, success is not a destination but an ongoing journey of learning, innovation, and improvement. Embrace the challenges, celebrate the wins, and never stop striving for excellence in your online business endeavors.

The Online Entrepreneur:
Your Comprehensive Guide to Building a Successful Business Online

CHAPTER 11:

EMBRACING THE ONLINE BUSINESS JOURNEY

As we come to the end of this book, it's time to reflect on the journey we have taken to explore the world of online business. Throughout this book, we have delved into various aspects of building a successful online business, from establishing a solid foundation to overcoming challenges and embracing growth. In this final chapter, we will recap the key insights and lessons learned, empowering you to embark on your online business journey with confidence and determination.

1. *Building a Strong Foundation*: We began by laying the groundwork for your online business, emphasizing the importance of defining your mission, vision, and values. We discussed the significance of understanding your target audience, conducting market research, and developing a compelling brand identity. By establishing a strong foundation, you set the stage for future success.

2. *Developing Effective Strategies*: Next, we explored the strategies and techniques necessary for online business growth. We discussed the significance of digital marketing, including search engine optimization (SEO), social media marketing, and content creation. We delved into the importance of customer engagement, effective communication, and data-driven decision-making. By implementing these strategies, you can reach and connect with your target audience more effectively.

3. *Overcoming Challenges*: No entrepreneurial journey is without challenges, and the online business world is no exception. We

addressed common obstacles faced by online entrepreneurs, such as market competition, technology barriers, and customer acquisition. We provided practical solutions and emphasized the importance of adaptability, perseverance, and a growth mindset. By adopting these principles, you can overcome challenges and transform them into opportunities for growth.

4. *Sustaining Long-Term Success*: Building a successful online business is not just about initial growth; it's about sustaining long-term success. We explored the significance of continuous learning, staying informed about industry trends, and adapting to market changes. We emphasized the value of building strong customer relationships, delivering exceptional experiences, and fostering a culture of innovation. By prioritizing sustainability and maintaining a customer-centric approach, you can ensure the continued growth and success of your online business.

Now you are equipped with the knowledge, strategies, and inspiration to embark on your online business journey. Remember, building a successful online business requires dedication, resilience, and a willingness to learn and adapt. Embrace the challenges as opportunities for growth and view setbacks as stepping stones to success.

Continuously seek new knowledge, stay connected with industry experts and fellow entrepreneurs, and remain passionate about your vision. Embrace innovation, prioritize customer satisfaction, and never stop striving for excellence.

Now is the time to take action. Embrace the online business journey with confidence and determination. Dream big, set goals, and work diligently towards making your vision a reality. Your success awaits in the dynamic and limitless world of online business.

The Online Entrepreneur:
Your Comprehensive Guide to Building a Successful Business Online

Let the Grind Start.

www.ingramcontent.com/pod-product-compliance
Lightning Source LLC
Chambersburg PA
CBHW062238290526
45794CB00006B/2339